Reel It In

SALMON FISHING

Tina P. Schwartz

PowerKiDS
press

New York

To Brandon, the littlest fish in our family—with love, Mom

Published in 2012 by The Rosen Publishing Group, Inc.
29 East 21st Street, New York, NY 10010

First Edition

Editor: Amelie von Zumbusch
Book Design: Kate Laczynski

Photo Credits: Cover, p. 16 © Chris Cheadle/age fotostock; pp. 4–5 iStockphoto/ Thinkstock; p. 6 © Minden Pictures/SuperStock; pp. 7, 9 (bottom) © All Canada Photos/ SuperStock; p. 8 Bill Schaefer/Getty Images; p. 9 (top) © www.iStockphoto.com/LeeAnn Townsend; pp. 10, 13 (left, right), 14–15, 17, 18, 20, 22 Shutterstock.com; p. 11 Grant Faint/Getty Images; p. 12 © www.iStockphoto.com/Kevin Beasley; p. 19 (top) © www. iStockphoto.com/RonTech2000; p. 19 (left) © www.iStockphoto.com/Pumba1; p. 21 Robert F. Sisson/National Geographic/Getty Images.

Library of Congress Cataloging-in-Publication Data

Schwartz, Tina P., 1969–
 Salmon fishing / by Tina P. Schwartz. — 1st ed.
    p. cm. — (Reel it in)
 Includes index.
 ISBN 978-1-4488-6196-5 (library binding) — ISBN 978-1-4488-6351-8 (pbk.) — ISBN 978-1-4488-6352-5 (6-pack)
 1. Salmon fishing—Juvenile literature. I. Title.
 SH684.S39 2012
 799.17'56—dc23
                                        2011017723

Manufactured in the United States of America

CPSIA Compliance Information: Batch #WW12PK: For Further Information contact Rosen Publishing, New York, New York at 1-800-237-9932

CONTENTS

I Love Salmon!

Lots of people like to fish for salmon. This man caught a coho salmon while fishing in a river in Alaska.

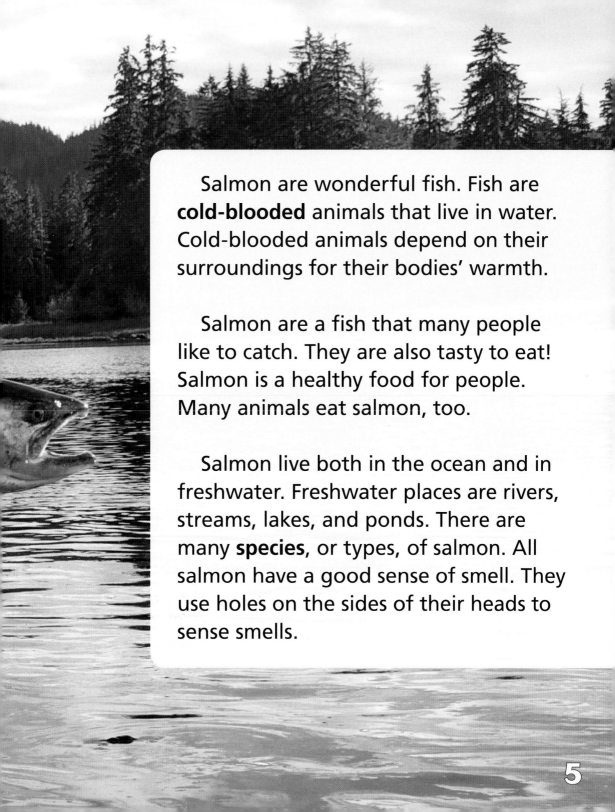

Salmon are wonderful fish. Fish are **cold-blooded** animals that live in water. Cold-blooded animals depend on their surroundings for their bodies' warmth.

Salmon are a fish that many people like to catch. They are also tasty to eat! Salmon is a healthy food for people. Many animals eat salmon, too.

Salmon live both in the ocean and in freshwater. Freshwater places are rivers, streams, lakes, and ponds. There are many **species**, or types, of salmon. All salmon have a good sense of smell. They use holes on the sides of their heads to sense smells.

The Amazing Life of Salmon

Salmon pass through stages as they grow. Newly hatched salmon are alevin. Alevin have yolk sacs that supply the food they need to grow. The orange part behind this alevin's head is its yolk sac.

Did you know that salmon are born in freshwater? All salmon start out as eggs. The eggs break open and tiny fish swim out.

Most young salmon **migrate**, or travel, to the ocean. It takes several months for the salmon to get there. As they travel to the ocean, the fish's bodies

change. These changes let the fish live in salt water. Salmon spend most of their lives feeding in the ocean.

In time, adult salmon swim back to the freshwater where they were born. They do this when it is time to **spawn**, or lay eggs. After they spawn, most salmon die.

These salmon have gathered to spawn in a stream in British Columbia. When many salmon swim upstream to spawn, it is called a salmon run.

Many Types of Salmon

Salmon can be found in both the Atlantic Ocean and the Pacific Ocean. Atlantic salmon are the only kind in the Atlantic Ocean. Chinook salmon, chum salmon, coho salmon, pink salmon, and sockeye salmon can be found on both sides of the Pacific Ocean. The cherry salmon lives only in Asia and parts of the Pacific Ocean near Asia.

Chinook salmon are also known as king salmon. They are the biggest of the species of salmon that live in the Pacific Ocean.

This young fisherman has caught a chum salmon. Chum salmon are known for their big, doglike teeth. In fact, they are sometimes called dog salmon.

Some salmon are raised on farms. These are not farms like those with cows and chickens. Salmon farms are also called fisheries. Only salmon are raised there. The farmers carefully control the water the fish live in and the food that they eat.

Salmon's bodies change when they return from the ocean to spawn in freshwater. For example, the parts of sockeye salmon behind their heads become bright red.

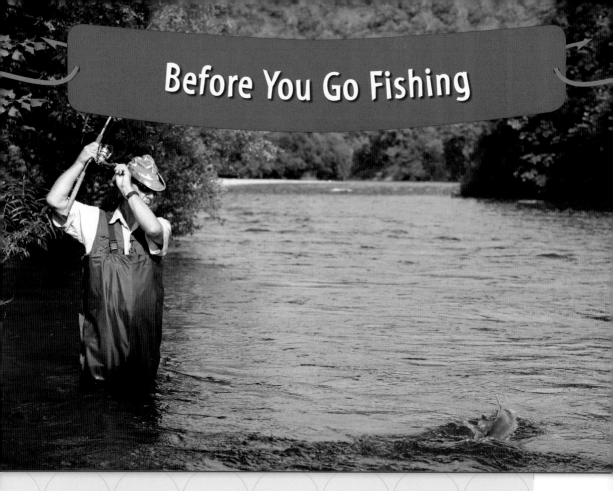

Before You Go Fishing

If you plan to fish in a shallow stream or river, consider wearing waders. These are overalls or pants that have boots as part of them. They keep you dry in the water.

Before you go fishing, you might need to get a **license**. This is a special paper that allows you to catch fish. There are two kinds of licenses. One is for **recreational** fishing, or fishing people do for fun. The second type of license is for **commercial** fishing.

It lets people sell their fish. Fishing laws are different from state to state. Check if the state you are fishing in requires a license to fish for salmon.

When you go fishing, be sure to bring a hat, sunscreen, snacks, and plenty of water to drink. Bring a bucket or a net to bring your fish home in, too.

Remember to bring a life jacket if you plan to go salmon fishing on a boat. It is smart to wear a life jacket even if you know how to swim.

Salmon-Fishing Gear

There are several ways to catch salmon. Many people use fishing poles with **reels**, lines, and **bait**. A reel is a wheel that has line wrapped around it. Bait is something you use to get fish to come to you. It can be a worm or even a pretend fish, called a **lure**.

Salmon are big fish. You need a rod that is strong but bendable to catch them. You will need a longer rod if you are fishing for the larger species of salmon.

Some fly-fishing flies are made for catching certain kinds of fish. This fly was made to catch Atlantic salmon.

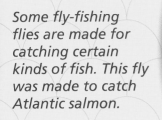

In fly-fishing, people use fishing flies as bait. These look a bit like real flies. They are made of string or feathers, though.

You start fishing by casting your line. To do this, pull your rod back. Then snap your wrist forward. This makes the line fly out in front of you.

There are many kinds of fishing reels. If you want to catch salmon, it is a good idea to use one that was made for salmon fishing, such as the one here.

Fishing in Freshwater

There are several ways to catch salmon in freshwater. One way is catch and release. In this method, you catch a fish and then let it go. This is done when people are fishing for fun instead of for something to eat.

Another way to fish in freshwater is spin casting. Spin casting is good for beginning **anglers**, or people who fish with a rod and reel. A spin-casting reel has a button on it that you push to release your line. Spin casting is a good way to catch small fish that you can cook in a pan.

This man is fly-fishing for salmon. Along with using flies instead of hooks and bait, poll use special rods for fly-fishing. Casting takes extra skill in fly-fishing, too.

Fishing in the Ocean

These boys caught a chinook salmon off Vancouver Island, British Columbia. In the ocean, chinook salmon are silver with bluish-green backs. When they return to freshwater, they turn other colors.

Fishing in the ocean can be harder than freshwater fishing. Salmon put up more of a fight in salt water. The water in the ocean often has bigger waves, too. These waves may make your fishing trip bumpier.

Try to fish along the shore when the tide is moving. When you fish in a shallow place, the incoming tide will bring in salmon from deeper water.

The best time to fish is at dawn, at dusk, or on cloudy, overcast days. The worst time to fish is when the weather is changing.

Resurrection Bay, Alaska, is a great place to catch salmon. Several species of salmon are found there. The bay is best known as a place to fish for coho salmon, though.

Yum! How to Prepare Your Catch

You have caught a fish, but now what? Ask a grown-up to remove the fish's head and insides and clean this fish.

One way to cook your salmon is on the grill. You can start by wrapping the salmon in a piece of foil. Next cover the fish with salt, pepper, spices, and

This man caught a big salmon while fishing off the coast of British Columbia. He can use it to feed a whole party of people!

Many people like eating sushi or sashimi made from salmon. This fish is not cooked, so it must be very fresh. It has to be prepared properly, too.

There are many ways to grill salmon. Some people grill salmon in foil packets, while others put it straight on a grill.

lemon juice. Then fold the foil around it. Have a grown-up put it on the grill and cook it.

A different way to fix your salmon is to brush egg over it and dip it in breadcrumbs. Then you can bake it in the oven. This will make your fish nice and crispy!

19

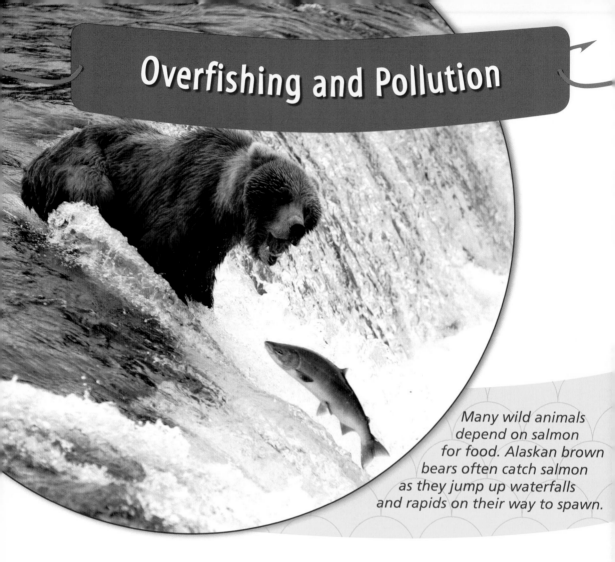

Overfishing and Pollution

Many wild animals depend on salmon for food. Alaskan brown bears often catch salmon as they jump up waterfalls and rapids on their way to spawn.

When too many people fish in one place, there will not be enough fish. This is known as overfishing. People sometimes **stock**, or add fish to, rivers and lakes that have been overfished. People may also pass laws that limit how many fish can be caught. In time, fish **populations**, or numbers, grow again.

Pollution in the water also kills fish. Pollution is waste made by people. People sometimes dump waste into waters. Pollution also washes into lakes and rivers after storms. From there, it flows into the oceans. People are now working to clean up water pollution. It is still a problem, though.

These scientists are rounding up sockeye salmon in British Columbia's Shuswap Lake to tag them. This will let the scientists track the fish's movements and learn more about them.

21

Smart Salmon Fishing

Salmon fishing is a big business. Due to this, salmon have been overfished in some places. In other places, such as the Alaska Panhandle, people have been careful not to overfish. There, salmon should feed people and supply fishing jobs for a long time.

This boy is holding a salmon he caught while fishing in the ocean. Whether you go fishing in freshwater or salt water, salmon fishing is lots of fun.

Do not be wasteful when you go salmon fishing. Consider using the catch and release method. If you catch more salmon than you can use, freeze the extra fish or give them away. Salmon are too tasty to waste!

GLOSSARY

anglers (ANG-glerz) People who fish with a rod and reel.

bait (BAYT) Something that is used to draw in animals being fished or hunted.

cold-blooded (KOHLD-bluh-did) Having body heat that changes with the heat around the body.

commercial (kuh-MER-shul) Having to do with business or trade.

license (LY-suns) Official permission to do something.

lure (LUHR) A fish-shaped object used for bait.

migrate (MY-grayt) To move from one place to another.

pollution (puh-LOO-shun) Man-made wastes that harm Earth's air, land, or water.

populations (pop-yoo-LAY-shunz) Groups of animals or people living in the same place.

recreational (reh-kree-AY-shnul) Having to do with something that is for fun, a hobby.

reels (REELZ) Things around which line or thread is wound.

spawn (SPAWN) To lay eggs.

species (SPEE-sheez) One kind of living thing. All people are one species.

stock (STOK) To refill the supply of something.

INDEX

WEB SITES

Due to the changing nature of Internet links, PowerKids Press has developed an online list of Web sites related to the subject of this book. This site is updated regularly. Please use this link to access the list:
www.powerkidslinks.com/reel/salmon/